WAR DOVE

Troy Cabida (b. 1995) is a Lc
former member of the Barbican Young Poets and the Roundhouse
Poetry Collective, and a producer for open mic night Poetry and
Shaah. His poems have appeared in TAYO, harana, Bukambibig, Cha
and Macmillan. War Dove is his debut pamphlet.

War Dove

Published by Bad Betty Press in 2020
www.badbettypress.com

Cover design by Amy Acre

Printed and bound in the United Kingdom

A CIP record of this book is available from the British Library.

ISBN: 978-1-913268-08-4

Supported using public funding by
**ARTS COUNCIL
ENGLAND**

LOTTERY FUNDED

War Dove

PRESS

Sumisilip ang umaga sa'king isip
At lumipas sa paggising
Ala-ala ng iyong tinig

– Ben&Ben

War Dove

Contents

Ladlad

From Tagalog – unfolded; spreading out on a surface; to expose;

and the nearest translation you're given is sharp,
translates to you stretching
out of yourself, your wrists bending
at the sides of a box struggling to contain you,
translates to you falling from somewhere high,
reminder that you are unpolished quartz,
your sense of man cracked for wanting man
as if to say:
you deserve all that is twisting your heart,
all that is crushing your torso.

Hawk and dove

Your favourite story
was when I tried to punch you
with a hand boxed like a rock
only to see it crack open on impact.
Fist bouncing from chest,
feather meeting concrete.

My favourite stories
were quiet ones that slipped through
your teeth, the way I caught
flickers of your eyes from mine to the ground.
The parts of you that needed defining
and how I once tried.

Makeup and Heels and Reece King

If the library manager assigns you the LGBTQ+ shelf
because you have 'specialist knowledge',
it's not your fault.

If they ask for your thoughts
on makeup and heels and Reece King,
it's not your fault (though you'll secretly Google Reece King after).

If they ask you for your pangalan sa gabi,
your name at night, the name you call yourself
when they're not around to remember and compare,
it's not your fault.

If they flash you and then retort
please it was just a joke don'tthinkofitthatway,
it's not your fault.

If the added weight
dumped into your backpack
is too heavy for their shoulders to carry,
it's not your fault.

If you can't see past all your smog,
you just can't see right now,
it's not your fault.

The Afters of After

In this week's episode of *Sorry For Your Loss*,
Leigh realises that she, too,
has become blind to other people's pain,
questioning the competence of her Type A personality.

*

My parents look relieved. Finally they get to talk, their tongues
marinated and their stories boiled for an easy chew. Finally they see
me sitting in front of them, home early for the first time in weeks.
The kitchen moist from steam and cigarette smoke and white wine.
They refer to a friend's son, whose name was meant for me. Paul.
Remember him? He works in Malta now. He's bisexual, too!

*

From the other end of the platform
you feel his heat and confidence.
White shirt, black slacks, white shoes.
Wonder what's hiding underneath.
He sits next to you, confirming
that you're a major character in God's sitcom.
He waits for your next move.

Buddy

He moulds a hand into my right shoulder
to soften the nervous muscle,

the friction between open mouth and stubbled cheek
revealing the truth in how much I've learnt

to find pleasure in the things that fight back.
I explore his tall, his swimmer lean,

enjoy touch as in gentle not penetrating,
let my body be a Friday afternoon.

In between exhales he calls me
stupid names like bro or buddy

as part of the experiment,
to be a sounding board of sorts,

to help make peace with old faces
who couldn't possibly give back.

Bonds

The poem is your personal definition of incompatibility.
Include a reference to a season. —Oscar James Boal

2017

We're zooming into a screen
small enough to fit the hand, its loudness
spilling through the room.

Winter sunlight splashes onto the screen
at the most awkward times,
catching our faces so focused

on their rhythm,
their flow of bodies as one, yes,
this is all they need. There is no difficulty.

He notices silence thickening in the room.
A beat passes, and then he exhales
Man, I have a feeling

we're not watching the same thing.
But you know that already. No point in falling
if there's no one to catch you on the other side.

Debris from Healing

Between Earls Court and Shadwell
I'm listening to She's Only Sixteen sing
about the parts that die as debris from healing.
They're singing so woefully
as if to throw away anything
no longer breathing is a bad thing,
as if to heal is a bad thing
but that's only your heart talking, the brain
left somewhere in the swirl of a five am cup of coffee,
inside a plastic bag waiting on a drunk person,
somewhere in the bus stop,
rolling around the first pile of fallen leaves
eager for summer to fizzle out.

Between Shadwell and Earls Court
I remember Jacob telling me
that if a line feels off, if the body
can function without it, simply pull.

Interlude: Calico

A male calico cat sits inside a room
full of dogs. Easily he sees through
their hunger, their boisterous and barrier.
He wants to let them know

but the room's already losing its sobriety
so instead he paws his way out,
feels the needles gnawing at a bent leg
dissolve like bubbles.

Outside, he looks to the sky
for a fast wind to catch
more of the citrus sunshine
clinging onto a fading summer,

drops to the ground
any leftover sting like balls of quartz:
firming the first bounce,
the eventual shatter

Examples of Confusion

I.
To the friends waiting on another day of happy.
Of maintaining that happy. Eating out with that happy.
Let that happy mimic the winter sun,
scorch down on you until you're numb,
capital H like a yellow ladder balancing itself.
You can laugh through floods and earthquakes and dictators
but your heart cracks easy for emotions? You're losing colour.

II.
I was in a Costa one Sunday morning editing
a friend's essay on depression when blankly she says
People like us don't go through things like this, do we?

Somewhere in Manila
a morning school bus leaves a housewife behind,
her husband on the last tricycle to work.
She tends to last night's beer bottle shards
lingering outside the front terrace,
sweeps them underneath a greying rug.

III.
The camera is practically making out
with Timothée Chalamet's face,
enjoying every inch of teary cheek,
romancing yet another scrunched up white boy forehead.
His words ooze out of his pores, thick like lava,
I swear I can taste him speak.

Lovechild

Along with Diana and Donna,
she carries with her a bit of Chaka
sways to a whole lot of Aretha. She roots for Beyoncé
and Janelle, calls them tomorrow's salvation,
exhales loudly at people from her generation
who disagree, who think they know everything
because they've seen everything

like   no, she won't be getting back in her box
           no, she won't move so you better cross the road
           no, she doesn't care if you report her
           yes, she could then and she still can now

like a prayer
from 3-11

have you got a Nectar card have you got Nectar a Nectar card
would you like a bag have you got Nectar would you like a receipt
thankyouverymuchnext next next next

War Dove

I.
The tenderness that can be achieved
in firming the world's many beatings,
in uprooting necessary truths out of yourself,
in driving yourself so far from sane and still
you are to bounce back solid.

II.
In front of the face that knows only one-sided healing,
I've come to know the kind of tender
that packs muscle, that doesn't cower
even to my own desires.
In front of the face that profits from my labour
but doesn't know how to give back,
the doves around me fought to remain.

III.
Much has been said about forgiveness
yet no one has managed to expound
the technical requirements necessary
to make the execution successful for both parties,
such as the understanding of the apology,
the need for it to be verbalised and accepted
to release the victim of their past, which can explain
why many find this a tricky action to perform,
like softening hardened honey,
crystallised and unflinching.

Calatagan, 2019

The kids are already laughing by the shores
giddy to pick the best starfish
but I'm still outside reception
standing in front of a small wishing pond
where white Mother Mary looks down
on brown and brass coins holding wishes
she'll decide when to play into reality.
Three turtles are balancing on top of one another
on a chunk of cement peeping from the water.
A fourth is a little away to the left
hiding from Mary's blessings, as if saying
no, I'm not ready for your light,
let me soak a little longer,
take up a form of healing
with the floating rust and petals,
searching for something that might still be useful

Phonetic

Tagalog is a tactile being,
arms and feet familiar to earth and sun,
to years of toil and exhaustion.

It doesn't recognise gender.
There is no he or she, just siya.
It doesn't care for silent endings,

no vowel unused, no consonant unpronounced,
it is a meal we consume to the bone
like whole roast pig and fried milk-fish eyes.

Sarcasm chewed through the crunch.
We speak and we are full.
Through this, we inherit a sober mentality:

Get your idea out there. Move on to the next.
Hands are meant for doing. Creases will smoothen.
Malayo naman iyan sa bituka. Not the end of the world.

You are either on top trying to stay on top
or at the bottom, waiting for the wheel
to take you back up.

According to my father, this is why
Filipinos can laugh through floods.
We're taught to believe that sooner or later
water dries up.

In Conversation with Past Troy

I have run around with your grief
like a stone in my pocket,
piercing a denimed thigh
to remind me that it exists,
that as long as the body is moving
the heart will follow. Now,
this technique will make you short circuit,
make you spill and slip into poems and empty bottles
and angry good morning texts on days you don't come home.
You will discover people's reaction to danger.
You will lose the heart to hearts,
the arguments about aliens, the random road trips
and texts for beer. You will learn to heal wounds
by kissing, learn that kisses don't always heal.
You will talk to your dad more,
check in with your mom more.
You will apologise with more of your chest
and then understand that you have a chest
and legs and dick and hands all itching for progress.
You will swallow pride until it no longer stings.
Your skeleton will toughen, grow muscle
from the bone upwards,
gathering strength to start cleaning the city.

Interviewing Marilyn, 1955

Her expressions, like a body of water,
her words, feather offerings to the wind.

She's wishing for no more heavy jewellery,
airplane rushes and midnight arguments

that spike upon landing. She's going to treat people
as she wants to be treated: her new form of prayer.

Awkward at first, but the plan here
is to seek freedom inside a chrysalis,

heal from butterfly to caterpillar,
sure and solid of self,

the brim overflowing
with all kinds of tomorrow.

Not Dying for London

not   as in denial/as in resistance as a physical form of
denial/as in growing older/as in growing in the right tempo/as in
tightness around my stomach/as in exhales that do nothing/as in
this isn't what should be defined as healing

dying   as in Sunday evenings talking to a bridge/as in
rejecting a hug/as in a sleeping drunk/as in your back as a symphony
of cracks/as in the path I chose/as in a side effect of truth/as in a
side effect of silence/as in not speaking

for   as in empathy/as in the lesser sibling of
compassion/as in service for others/as in disservice to the self/as in
going through with it/as in deflecting bullets/as in by refusing my
embrace, whose heart are you really protecting

London   as in white woman shoulder bumping into me/as
in strong pace to deflect white woman shoulder bumping into me/
as in every day delay/as in every day diverted/as in blind when rainy
but blinding when sunny/as in weather trying to kill me/as in a city
trying to kill me/as in a city trying to toughen me up/as in a city
trying to kill me/as in a city failing

Notes

'Interlude: Calico' is after 'Serendipity' by BTS.

'Lovechild' is for Aline Sylvester (but she knows that already).

'War Dove' is after 'Trevor' by Ocean Vuong.

'Phonetic' is after 'MOTHER TONGUES', an intergenerational poetry, film and translation project celebrating the work of acclaimed poets of colour alongside the cultures, languages and women who've nurtured them by Victoria Adukwei Bulley.

'Interviewing Marilyn, 1955' is after a television interview between Marilyn Monroe and Ed Murrow, discussing Monroe's independence from 20th Century Fox and the conception of Marilyn Monroe Productions. It is also after a sonnet by Terrance Hayes describing James Baldwin's face.

'Not dying for London' is written after a form Jeremiah Brown created called the Ogden.

Acknowledgements

'Ladlad' was first published in *harana poetry* (June 2019).

'Bonds' was published in *TAYO Literary Magazine* (June 2019).

'Examples of confusion' was first published in *Voice & Verse Poetry Magazine* (September 2018).

'Not dying for London' is forthcoming in *SLAM! You're Gonna Wanna Hear This* by Macmillan (September 2020).

Thank you to Amy Acre and Jake Wild Hall. May long you continue giving poems a home outside of notebooks and open mic nights.

To Jacob Sam-La Rose for absolutely everything. To Rachel Long, Kat Lahr, Nazmia Jamal, Jennifer Ogole, Bridget Minamore and Cecilia Knapp. To R.A. Villanueva and Romalyn Ante, aking mga kapatid. To Amina Jama, Gabriel Jones, Christy Ku, Sean Mahoney, Esme Allman, The Repeat Beat Poet, Helen Bowell, Natalie Linh Bolderston, Kelly Roberts, Jeremiah Brown, Laurie Ogden and Gabriel Akamọ. To Fahima Hersi, Abdullahi Mohammed, Idil Abdullahi, my #rideordie Ayaan Abdullahi and Neimo Askar, my heart.

To Zyrlyn-ssi and Boss Man Joshua. To Madam Judylyn, Coach G Jelyn and Queen Mami Ate Jyds. To Tita Eden. To CJ. To Kuya Mark. To Nichola, Carlotta, Vicky, James, John, Matt, Claudine and

Rachael. To William. To Miguel and Stacy. To Marie. To Hannah. To Aira, GJ and Angel. To Eva Noblezada. To Janelle Monáe. To Haley Reinhart. To Amy Winehouse. To Karylle. To V. To Jimin.

To Vaughn, Claire and Mischa for your love. To Ate Aiya for your strength. To Ate Michelle for your warmth. To Ate Selene for your light. To my Mom for my ascendant in Capricorn. To my Dad for your award-winning fried rice. I love you all.

To Sang'gre Alena. To Elio Perlman. To Leigh Shaw. To Jo March. To David and Adrian. To Diana Prince.

To God, Your angels and Your weird sense of humour.

New and recent titles from Bad Betty Press

At the Speed of Dark
Gabriel Akamo

bloodthirsty for marriage
Susannah Dickey

poems for my FBI agent
Charlotte Geater

No Weakeners
Tim Wells

The Body You're In
Phoebe Wagner

Blank
Jake Wild Hall

*And They Are Covered
in Gold Light*
Amy Acre

Alter Egos
Edited by Amy Acre
and Jake Wild Hall

She Too Is a Sailor
Antonia Jade King

Raft
Anne Gill

While I Yet Live
Gboyega Odubanjo

The Death of a Clown
Tom Bland

Forthcoming in 2020

Animal Experiments
Anja Konig

A Terrible Thing
Gita Ralleigh

Sylvanian Family
Summer Young

Rheuma
William Gee

Lightning Source UK Ltd.
Milton Keynes UK
UKHW011846130420
361645UK00001B/77

9 781913 268084